WORKBOOK

—— of ——

THE
TOOLS

By
Spark Notes

This book cannot be reproduced or stored in a retrieval system without the permission of the publisher, except for purposes such as back review and research.

This is an unofficial workbook of "The Tools" created to enrich your reading experience.

The information herein has been provided for informational, educational and entertainment purposes only.

Copyright ©, 2023
All rights reserved

THIS WORKBOOK
BELONGS TO:

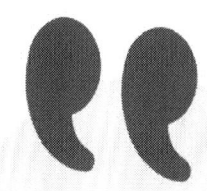

"Real change requires you to change your behavior–not just your attitude."

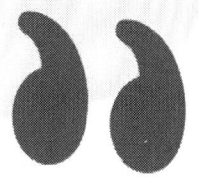

— PHIL STUTZ

Transform Your Problems into Courage, Confidence, and Creativity through
"THE TOOLS"

« THE TOOLS » provides practical exercises and strategies for accessing the power of your inner self in order to overcome any challenge and create the life you desire. The authors offer simple yet effective tools that can be used to transform fear and anxiety into courage, to increase self-confidence, and to foster creativity. Through this book, readers can learn to access the power of their inner self, allowing them to unlock their potential and create the life they have always dreamed of.

Let's get started...

Table of Contents

About the book.. 8
Why do we need the tools ? 9
Tool #1:the reversal of desire.................... **10**
1. Focus on your pain 12
2. Move toward the pain................................ 14
3. Freedom... 16
Tool #2:active love 18
1. Concentration 20
2. Transmission... 22
3. Penetration... 24
Tool #3:inner authority.................................... 26
1. Imagine you are on stage........................... 28
2. Shout, "LISTEN!" 30
Tool #4: the grateful flow............................ 32
1. List what you're grateful for....................... 34
2. Feel the sensation of gratefulness. 36
3. Connect to the source................................ 38
Tool #5: jeopardy... 40
1. Deathbed scene... 42
2. Scream at yourself..................................... 44
3. Use fear as a motivator.............................. 46
Journal... 48

About The Book

Phil Stutz and Barry Michels bring forward a new approach to self-help in their book « The Tools ».

This book not only comes with powerful tools and strategies that can assist in personal development, but also includes many personal stories from the authors, outlining their successes and failures when it comes to putting these tools into practice. It also offers readers a unique spiritual look at the world and its psychotherapy, with the concept of "Higher Forces" playing a major role in helping people become creators of their own destiny. This book is a must-have for anyone looking to start their journey of self-discovery, as it provides detailed insight into the intricate relationships between one's psychology and spirituality. It offers a comprehensive guide for those in need of direction and healing, and is sure to open the door to a brighter future for its readers.

Why do we need the tools?

Having the right attitude and the desire to change your life are both valuable components in life, but they are not enough to bring about the desired results. We must take the necessary actions in order to see the resultes we hope to achieve. This is where the tools presented in the book are invaluable.

They provide us with a practical way to tackle the common issues we all encounter. By using these tools and connecting to something greater than ourselves (as the authors refer to as "Higher Forces"), we can consistently move forward and unlock our true potential.

With this new found connection to the "Higher Forces", we can develop a renewed sense of purpose and strength, enabling us to grow and progress in life. As we use these tools and techniques more often, we can become more in tune with our inner selves, helping us to identify our creativity and potential. As we move forward, we can unlock our true potential and use our newfound power to create positive change in our own lives and the lives of those around us.

Tool #1:
The Reversal of Desire

The Higher Force: Forward Motion

We all tend to avoid facing difficult situations and emotions in life, as they can be painful and challenging. However, this approach keeps us limited and prevents us from reaching our true potential. If we want to live our best lives, we must learn to "reverse our desire" and get out of our Comfort Zone.

Rather than trying to shirk away from pain, we should welcome it as an opportunity for growth and development. The old saying of "No pain, no gain" applies here, as only when we confront our fears and push ourselves out of our Comfort Zone can we truly make progress. The cost of avoiding pain is a life full of regret, so the next time you are faced with a difficult task, challenge, or emotion, practice the following steps

Keywords

Actions To take

Let's practice

1 FOCUS ON YOUR PAIN

Facing your pain can be daunting, and it's easy to want to avoid it. But if you want to reach your true potential, you must learn to confront your fears and accept your pain.

To do this, it can help to focus on the pain you are avoiding and visualize it appearing in front of you in the form of a cloud. Only then you can express your desire for the pain, recognizing that it has great value and can help you to grow and develop. When you face your pain head-on, you can access its powerful energy and use it to propel yourself forward.

Keywords

Actions To take

2. MOVE TOWARD THE PAIN
silently scream, "I love pain!" as you keep moving forward. By expressing your love for the pain, you can begin to open yourself up to it and move so deeply into the pain that you become one with it. This can help you to access the powerful energy of pain, which can be used to propel you forward on your journey. Instead of being overwhelmed by the fear of pain, you can learn to love it and use it to your advantage.

Keywords

Actions To take

3. FREEDOM

After facing the pain you are avoiding, it's important to give yourself permission to move on. To do this, you can visualize the cloud spitting you out and closing behind you. As you leave the cloud, you can say inwardly, "Pain sets me free!" This can remind you that by confronting your pain, you open up a realm of pure light and freedom. As you move away from the cloud of pain, you can feel yourself being propelled forward. you can use this powerful energy to continue your journey of growth and development.

Keywords

Actions To take

Tool #2:
Active Love

The Higher Force: Outflow

When you're feeling angry or frustrated, it can be easy to get stuck in a loop of rumination and thought. you can get lost in a mental maze, spinning our wheels and allowing your anger and frustration to consume you. It's important to recognize when this is happening and take steps to get out of the maze.

One way to do this is to invite mindfulness to notice when you're stuck in the maze. you can use this recognition to check in with yourself and ask: Is this serving me? Is this thought process leading me to a solution? If the answer is no, you can choose to step out of the maze and focus on finding a positive solution. you can remind yourself that when you are stuck in the maze, life passes you by. you can choose to use your energy and time wisely and focus on finding a solution instead of spinning your wheels and getting stuck in rumination.

Keywords

Actions To take

Let's practice

1. CONCENTRATION

Step one of connecting to the Higher Force is to practice concentration. Begin by closing your eyes and taking several deep, calming breaths. Visualize your heart expanding outward in all directions, encompassing the world of infinite love that surrounds you. Feel yourself being filled with the energy of love and light. When your heart contracts back to its normal size, you will be left with a concentrated source of love and light inside your chest. Allow yourself to be filled with confidence and courage as you focus on this energy and its power to propel you forward.

Keywords

Actions To take

2. TRANSMISSION

Step two of connecting to the Higher Force is to practice transmission. Visualize the love and light that is concentrated in your chest extending outwards to the other person. Feel the energy of love and understanding transmitting itself from you to the other person. Allow yourself to be filled with compassion and understanding as you transmit this energy of love and light. Know that whatever the outcome, you have done your best to reach out in a spirit of understanding and kindness.

Keywords

Actions To take

3. PENETRATION

Step three of connecting to the Higher Force is to practice penetration. As you send the love and light from your chest, imagine it entering the other person and filling them with love and understanding. Sense a oneness between you and them, feeling the energy of love and understanding connecting you both. Then, relax and allow all of the energy that you have given away to return to you. Feel the power of the Higher Force that connects us all, and be thankful for the peace and love that it brings.

Keywords

Actions To take

Tool #3:
Inner Authority

The Higher Force: Self-Expression

Next time you feel anxious due to a challenging situation, such as speaking in front of a group or asking your boss for a pay raise, take a few moments to acknowledge your Shadow. Acknowledge the parts of yourself that you fear the most and take some moments to sit with those feelings. Allow yourself to feel the discomfort and, in doing so, you will be able to move forward and confront your fears with greater strength, courage, and confidence.

As you confront your fears, use deep breathing and visualizations to calm your mind and body. Visualize yourself in the scenario, your anxieties and fears, and imagine yourself feeling confident, courageous, and ready to take on the challenge. By connecting with your Shadow and confronting your anxieties, you will find a source of strength and courage that will help you to show up with authority and confidence in any situation.

Keywords

Actions To take

Let's practice

1. IMAGINE YOU ARE ON STAGE

Step one of confronting your Shadow is to take a few moments to close your eyes and imagine yourself standing in front of an audience, be It one or thousands of people. As you take this mental journey, focus completely on the Shadow and feel an unbreakable bond between you and the shadow. Visualize yourself feeling strong and fearless as a unit.

Take several deep breaths and allow yourself to sink into the moment. Imagine the courage and confidence you have within, and allow yourself to fully embrace it. Feel the strength of your connection to the Shadow, and to the audience before you. Remind yourself that you are ready, and that you are capable of achieving anything.

Keywords

Actions To take

2. SHOUT, "LISTEN!"

Step two is to imagine yourself and the Shadow turning forcefully toward the audience and commanding, with one voice, "LISTEN!" Feel the power and authority that comes with speaking with one voice. Allow yourself to channel the confidence and courage of the Shadow, freeing yourself from any anxiety and fear.

Take a few more deep breaths and embrace the courage and confidence that comes with speaking with authority. Feel the strength of your connection to the Shadow and to the audience before you. Now, you are ready to take on any challenge and present yourself with authority and confidence.

Keywords

Actions To take

Tool #4:
The Grateful Flow

The Higher Force: The Source

When those dark, negative thoughts start to consume your mind, the Black Cloud takes over. It stifles the potential of your life and withholds the best of you from your loved ones. Rather than living to fulfill a great promise, life becomes a struggle to merely survive.

Feeling overwhelmed and like you are surrounded by a black cloud? It's time to connect to the source of your strength and get your grateful flow on.

Start by acknowledging the amazing things in your life. Even if it's just one small thing, give thanks for it and feel the gratitude fill you. When your mind starts to wander off and think negative thoughts, take a moment to remember the good things in your life and appreciate them. Whenever you feel overwhelmed, take a few moments to reflect on the things you are thankful for, and the feeling of gratitude will be sure to ground you.

Keywords

Actions To take

Let's practice

1. LIST WHAT YOU'RE GRATEFUL FOR

Take your time to silently reflect on the things in your life that you are grateful for—especially the little things that you tend to take for granted. As you list each item, take the time to really feel the gratitude and appreciation for it. Challenge yourself by not repeating the same items—stretch your list to include as many new items as possible.

List the things you're grateful for :

Keywords

Actions To take

2. FEEL THE SENSATION OF GRATEFULNESS.

Once you have listed about thirty seconds worth of items that you are grateful for, take the time to pause and relish in the physical sensation of gratefulness that can be felt coming directly from your heart. This energy that is generated is known as the Grateful Flow.

Keywords

Actions To take

3. CONNECT TO THE SOURCE

Connecting to the Source is an incredibly powerful, transformative experience. Through this connection, you can feel an overwhelming presence of infinite giving and unconditional love. Your heart will open and your chest will soften, allowing the energy to emanate from within. As you open up to the Source, you will experience a greater sense of peace, clarity, and joy - enabling you to live a life of purpose and abundance. This connection is truly a spiritual awakening and something that can be carried with you no matter what life may bring.

Keywords

Actions To take

Tool #5:
Jeopardy

The Higher Force: Willpower

It can be easy to fall into the trap of believing that you have "arrived" and no longer have to put in the work to maintain your success. This can lead to complacency and cause you to forget some of the most important Tools that you have used to get to where you are. One of the most essential Tools is the use of Jeopardy, which gives you the willpower and drive to stay in the game, even when facing setbacks or defeats. Jeopardy provides you with a way to stick with your practice and keep pushing yourself, even when the going gets tough. It also allows you to stay focused and motivated, so that you can continue to make progress and reach your goals.

Keywords

Actions To take

Let's practice

1. DEATHBED SCENE

As you lie on your deathbed, you may feel a sense of peace and acceptance as you reflect on your life, your accomplishments, and your failures. You can look back with gratitude for the moments, both big and small, that made up your life and perhaps, with a bit of hindsight, see how each of these moments, both good and bad, shaped you into the person you became. As your life comes to an end, you may feel a sense of fulfillment and contentment, knowing that you have lived a life that was true to who you are and that you have left the world a better place than you found it.

Keywords

Actions To take

2. SCREAM AT YOURSELF

As you look back on your life, you may find yourself wishing for a few more days, months, or even years to accomplish something meaningful or to spend some more time with those you love. In this moment, an older version of yourself may appear and scream at you to make the most of the present moment. This version of yourself reminds you to not take the time you have for granted, to seize the day and make the most of every single moment. The older version of yourself encourages you to take risks and not be afraid of failure, to dream big and aim high, and to never miss an opportunity to make a positive impact in the world.

Keywords

Actions To take

3. USE FEAR AS A MOTIVATOR

As you lie on your deathbed, you may feel a deep, hidden fear that you have been squandering your life and wasting the precious time you have been given. This fear may create an urgent desire within you to take advantage of every opportunity that comes your way and to use whatever tools are necessary in order to get the most out of every moment. This fear can be used as a powerful motivator to push you forward and to encourage you to never give up, no matter how difficult the task may be. By accepting this fear and using it as a source of motivation, you can make the most of every single second and create a life that you can be proud of.

Keywords

Actions To take

Journal

Made in the USA
Coppell, TX
04 December 2023

ISBN 9798377156178